YOU CAN TEACH YOURSELF FIDDLING

By Craig Duncan

This book has been designed for beginning students of fiddling. The 36 lessons present basic fiddling techniques by applying them to fiddle tunes. It is not necessary to know how to read music, as the lessons explain one step at a time, and fingerings are given for every note. Constant review should be done as the student works through the book, improving tunes that have been previously learned while adding new concepts. Many of the tunes are found in more that one lesson. Each version builds on the previous version and helps students see how to create their own arrangements of the tunes.

A VHS/DVD video of the music covering Lessons 1-17 is now available. The publisher strongly recommends the use of this resource along with the text to insure accuracy of interpretation and ease in learning. Although this series deals with self instruction, it is always helpful to have a teacher. It may prove very beneficial to have a violinist coach you on basic fundamentals if there is not a teaching fiddler in your area. You may even convert him/her to the joys of fiddling. I wish you a great success with the fiddling!

CD CONTENTS

1 Playing The Open Strings (:57)
2 The A Scale (1:36) **Lesson 2**
3 Mary Had A Little Lamb (:28)
4 Twinkle, Twinkle Little Star (:43)
5 Liza Jane (:33) **Lesson 3**
6 Camptown Races (:31)
7 Buffalo Gals (:40) **Lesson 4**
8 Shady Grove (:40)
9 Shortnin' Bread (:48) **Lesson 5**
10 Oh, Susanna (1:12)
11 Cindy (1:10)
12 The D Scale (:32) **Lesson 6**
13 Dixie (1:32)
14 Wildwood Flower (2:32) **Lesson 7**
15 Angeline The Baker (1:00)
16 Soldier's Joy (1:02)
17 Going To Boston (1:01) **Lesson 8**
18 The G Scale (:52) **Lesson 9**
19 Flop Eared Mule (1:09)
20 Skip To My Lou (:40) **Lesson 10**
21 The Girl I Left Behind Me (1:12)
22 The Fourth Finger (:45) **Lesson 11**
23 Bile Them Cabbage Down (1:19)
24 Old Joe Clark (1:13)
25 Up Jumped The Devil (:49) **Lesson 12**
26 Cripple Creek (:33)
27 Flop Eared Mule (:59)

28 Bile Them Cabbage Down (:54)
Lesson 13
29 Old Joe Clark (:49)
30 Up Jumped The Devil (:49) **Lesson 14**
31 Going To Boston (:52)
32 Mississippi Sawyer (1:14) **Lesson 15**
33 Soldier's Joy (1:13)
34 Flop Eared Mule (1:11) **Lesson 16**
35 Skip To My Lou (1:08)
36 Cripple Creek (:41) **Lesson 17**
37 Old Joe Clark (1:08)
38 Introductions (1:13) **Lesson 18**
39 Arkansas Traveler (1:03)
40 My Love She's But A Lassie (1:11)
Lesson 22
41 New Castle (1:08)
42 Southwind (1:16) **Lesson 23**
43 Si Bheag, Si Mhor (2:18)
44 The A Scale (:53) **Lesson 24**
45 Bile Them Cabbage Down (:30)
46 The Sandy River (:58)
47 Fine Times At Our House (1:00)
Lesson 25
48 Salt River (:57)
49 Mississippi Sawyer (1:03) **Lesson 26**
50 Chinky Pin Or Too Young To
Marry(1:02)

51 Cotton Eyed Joe (:51) **Lesson 27**
52 The Cameron Highlanders (1:57)
53 Scotland The Brave (1:24)
54 Harvest Home (1:05)
55 Ash Grove (1:14) **Lesson 29**
56 Amazing Grace (:40)
57 Miss Mcleod's Reel (:55) **Lesson 30**
58 Swinging On A Gate (1:04)
59 Fisher's Hornpipe (1:19) **Lesson 31**
60 Snowflake Reel (1:01)
61 Understanding Keys & Scales (:42)
Lesson 32
62 Key Of A-3 Sharps (:39)
63 Key Of B Flat-2 Flats (:38)
64 Key Of C (:36)
65 Key Of D (:37)
66 Key Of E (:38)
67 Key Of F (:38)
68 Double Shuffle (:20) **Lesson 33**
69 C & G Chord Double-Shuffle Exercise
(:50)
70 Back Up And Push (1:11)
71 Orange Blossom Shuffle (:43) **Lesson 34**
72 Rubber Dolly (:56)
73 Irish Washerwoman (:49) **Lesson 35**
74 Garry Owen (:49)
75 St. Patrick's Day (1:11)

Visit us on the Web at www.melbay.com — E-mail us at email@melbay.com

Contents

Alphabetical Listing of Tunes

Parts of the Fiddle

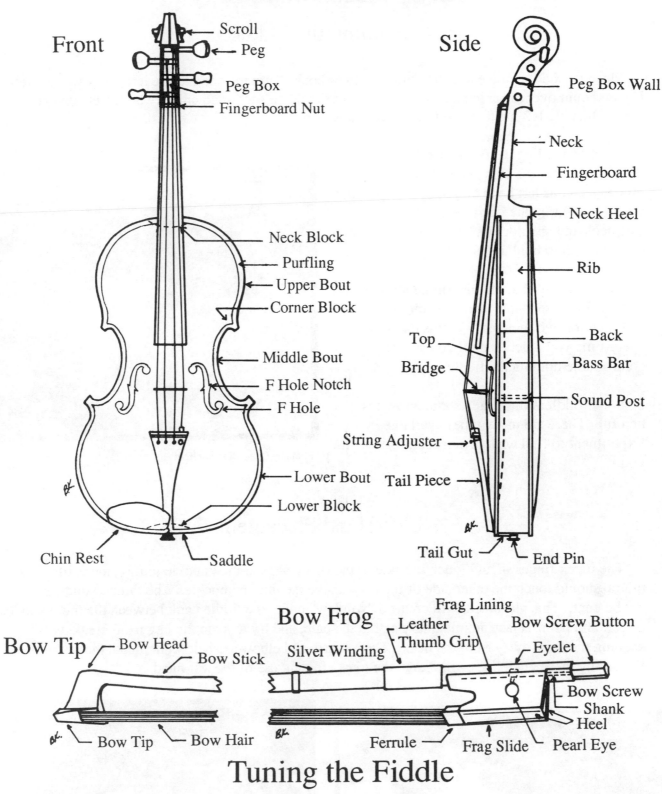

Front

- Scroll
- Peg
- Peg Box
- Fingerboard Nut
- Neck Block
- Purfling
- Upper Bout
- Corner Block
- Middle Bout
- F Hole Notch
- F Hole
- Lower Bout
- Lower Block
- Chin Rest
- Saddle

Side

- Peg Box Wall
- Neck
- Fingerboard
- Neck Heel
- Rib
- Back
- Top
- Bridge
- Bass Bar
- Sound Post
- String Adjuster
- Tail Piece
- Tail Gut
- End Pin

Bow Tip

- Bow Head
- Bow Stick
- Bow Tip
- Bow Hair

Bow Frog

- Frag Lining
- Leather
- Thumb Grip
- Silver Winding
- Bow Screw Button
- Eyelet
- Bow Screw
- Shank
- Heel
- Ferrule
- Frag Slide
- Pearl Eye

Tuning the Fiddle

The open strings of the fiddle are tuned by twisting the pegs and by adjusting the fine tuners. The pegs must be pushed in as they are turned, or they will slip. The screws on the fine tuners work like other types of screws: Turning clockwise makes the string tighter (higher), and turning counterclockwise makes the string looser (lower). The highest string is tuned to the second E above middle C. The second string is tuned to the A above middle C. The third string is tuned to the D, one step above middle C, and the lowest string is tuned to the G below middle C. These pitches may be matched to a piano, a tuning pipe, or other source. Several companies manufacture small quartz tuning devices which may prove very useful. Check with your local music store to find what best suits your needs.

Lesson 1
Holding the Fiddle

Place the fiddle on the left shoulder and collarbone. Turn the head to the left and lower the left jaw and chin over the chin rest. The instrument should be supported entirely by the chin and shoulder, so that the left hand is free to note the instrument.

Practice holding the fiddle parallel to the floor using only the chin and shoulder. To do this, place your left hand on your right shoulder while holding up the instrument. The neck and shoulder muscles should only be tight enough to hold up the fiddle.

Time yourself holding the fiddle with "no hands" for 30 seconds, then for a minute, and then for two minutes. Do this exercise every time you practice until you are very comfortable holding the fiddle.

Some fiddlers find that a shoulder rest is helpful. There are many types available. Experiment to find what is most comfortable for you.

Photo by Charmaine Lanham

Left-Hand Placement

The index finger should touch the side of the fiddle neck at the knuckle joining the palm. The thumb should touch the other side of the neck above the thumb knuckle. The thumb knuckle should not be bent. This placement will create a "window" under the fiddle neck between the thumb, index finger, and palm. Place an imaginary egg in the palm and try to keep the egg from breaking by keeping the palm away from the neck. The left arm and elbow are held underneath the instrument. Following these guidelines will assure the most efficient use of the left hand.

Photo by Charmaine Lanham

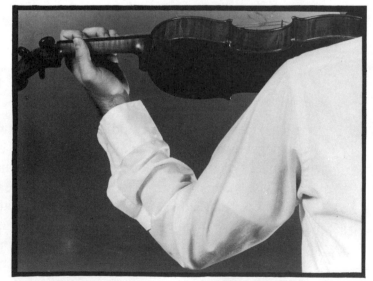

Photo by Charmaine Lanham

Holding the Bow

The first finger should touch the bow between the first and second joints. The middle and ring fingers should wrap around the bow comfortably, and the tip of the little finger should rest on the top edge of the bow. The fingers should be curved and spread apart. The thumb should be placed partially on the frog and partially on the stick, forming a circle with the middle finger. Always bend the thumb outward, as this eliminates excess tension in the right hand. The bow should be held with as little pressure as possible.

Practice finding the bow grip, checking your grip with the pictures of the correct position. Do this 20 times each practice session until it feels natural.

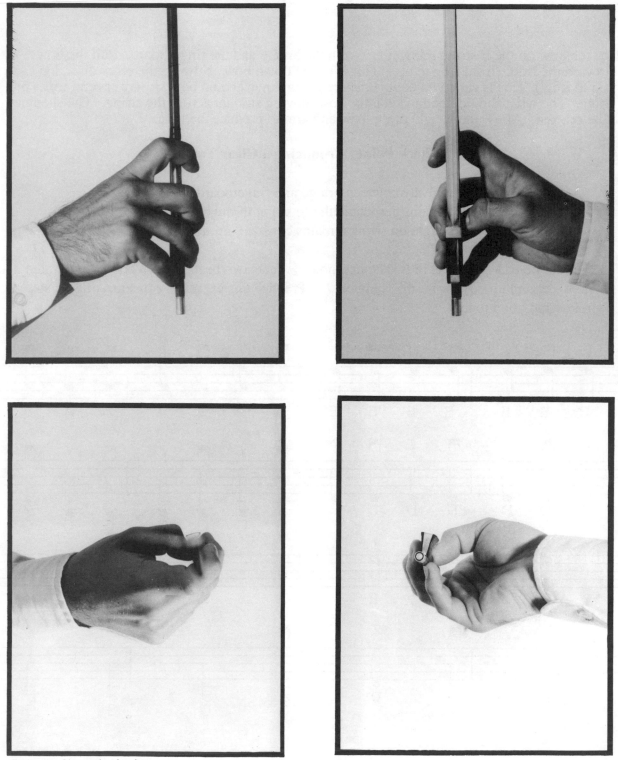

Photos by Charmaine Lanham

Playing the Open Strings

The names of the open strings from highest to lowest in pitch are E, A, D and G. They are notated on the following spaces of the treble clef.

Place the bow on the E string midway between the bridge and the fingerboard. Pull the bow down toward the floor (from frog to tip.) This is called down bow. Now go the other direction (from tip to frog.) This is called up bow. Practice going down and up bow slowly several times on each string. The wrist should bend to keep the bow moving straight across the string. The shoulder should be relaxed. Allow the weight of the bow and arm to produce the tone.

Check Point - Producing a Clear Tone

1. Bow midway between bridge and fingerboard.
2. Bow remains perpendicular to string throughout stroke.
3. Bow weight on string remains constant throughout stroke.

The quarter note ♩ gets one beat. The half note ♪ gets two beats. Down bows are marked with this symbol ⊓ and up bows with this symbol ∨. Practice this exercise, concentrating on straight bow strokes and good tone.

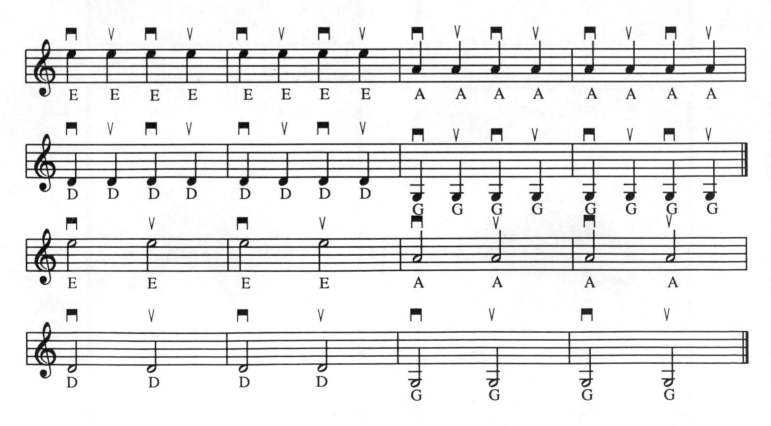

6

Lesson 2
The A Scale

Sharps raise the pitch by a half step, and flats lower the pitch by a half step. Naturals are notes that are neither sharps nor flats. The number of sharps or flats determines the key and the finger positions.

When three sharps are found at the beginning of the staff, the music is in the key of A. The sharps are F♯, C♯, and G♯. In this key the fingers are placed on the A and E strings like this diagram:

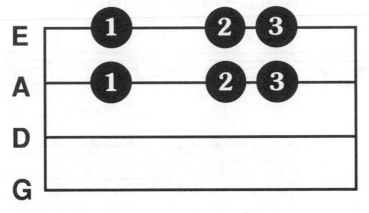

The fingertips should be able to touch one string at a time. Press firmly on the strings, but do not grip tightly. The left hand needs to be as relaxed as possible. Always use the tips of the fingers and remember the proper hand position

Check Point - Proper Hand Position

1. Index finger touching the fiddle neck at the lower knuckle.
2. Thumb straight, touching the fiddle neck above the knuckle.
3. "Window" visible under fiddle neck between thumb and index finger.
4. "Egg" in palm to keep palm away from the fiddle neck.
5. Arm and elbow under fiddle.
6. Fingertips touch strings from above.

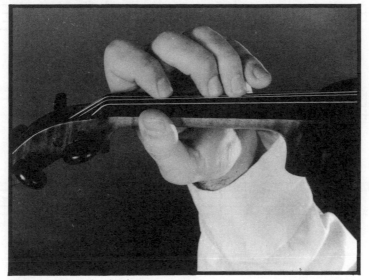

Photo by Charmaine Lanham

Play the following exercises starting on the A string, then place the first finger on the A string, then the second, followed by the third. After the third finger, go to the E string; then the first, the second, and the third fingers. The scale is then played in reverse.

The first finger should stay down when noting the second, and the first and second fingers should stay on the string when noting the third. Less hand movement makes for easier fiddling. Play slowly, concentrating on being in tune and producing a good tone.

A Scale - Quarter Notes

A Scale - Half Notes

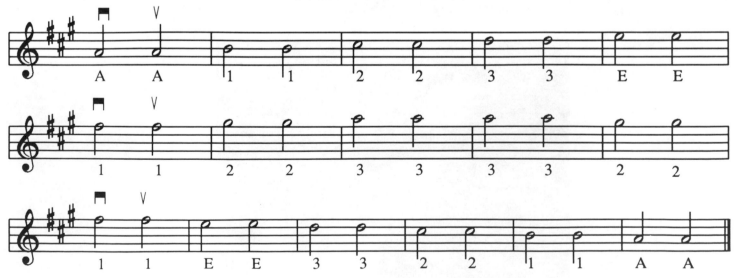

8

Now we will use the A scale to play two tunes that everyone has heard. Remember that the quarter notes get one beat, and the half notes get two beats. The last note in "Mary Had a Little Lamb" is a whole note, which receives four beats. The letters printed above the music are the guitar chords. Always keep proper hand and bow position in mind!

Mary Had a Little Lamb

Twinkle, Twinkle Little Star

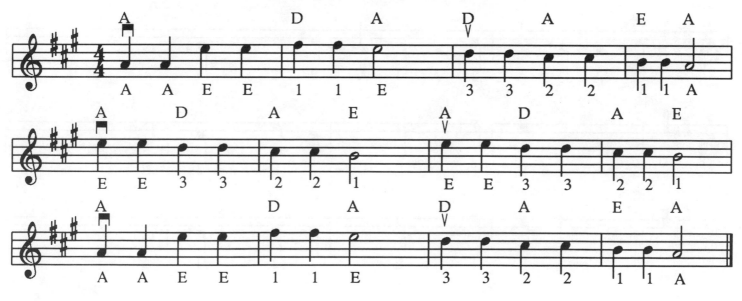

Lesson 3
The Dotted Half Note

When a dot is added after a note, the value or length of the note is increased by half. Remember the half note is equal to two beats. When it is followed by a dot, it is called a dotted half note and is now equal to three beats.

Check Point - Note Values

1. Quarter note   ♩   = one beat.
2. Half note   ♩   = two beats.
3. Dotted half note   ♩·   = three beats.
4. Whole note   o   = four beats.

The following tunes have each of the notes we have studied. Count carefully as you play.

Liza Jane

Camptown Races

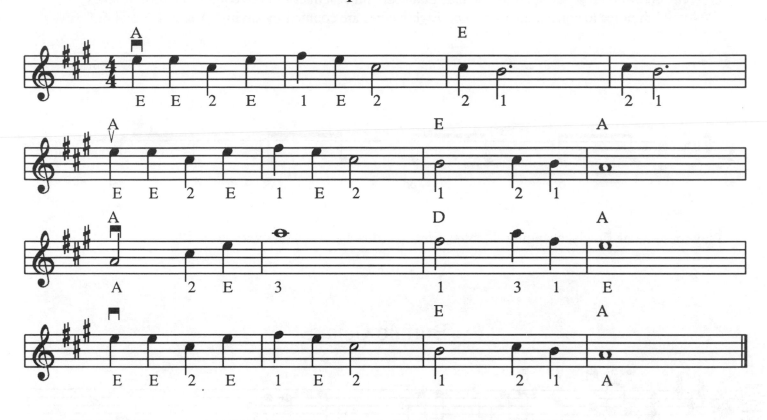

Review

1. Hold the fiddle up as you play, supporting it with your chin and shoulder. This helps free the left hand and positions the fiddle so that the bow can produce the best tone.
2. Keep your right thumb bent, forming a circle with the middle finger.
3. Keep the right "pinky" bent, with the tip of the finger on top of the bow. The other fingers should wrap around comfortably.
4. Watch the bow, keeping it between the bridge and the fingerboard.
5. Draw straight bow strokes with the bow, staying exactly perpendicular to the string. Be certain to play only one string at a time.
6. Check left-hand position for the "window" and the "egg."
7. Left elbow should be under the fiddle.
8. Play the scales and tunes in Lessons 2 and 3 from memory, watching yourself as you play.

Always keep proper position in mind. Good habits started early will make for easier playing.

Lesson 4
The Eighth Note

The eighth note ♪ is equal to one half of a beat. Since a quarter note equals one beat, it takes two eighth notes to equal a quarter note. Eighth notes are counted by saying "1 & 2 & 3 & 4 &."

Play these tunes slowly, changing the bow direction (down and up) on every note.

Buffalo Gals

"Shady Grove" is a modal tune which used the same finger spacing as the key of A. It sounds modal because it starts and ends on first-finger B instead of open A.

There is a comma at the end of the second line. This means to lift the bow so you will be ready for the following down bow.

Shady Grove

The Names of the Notes in the A Scale

So far we have played everything by finger number. All of the notes also have letter names. Memorize the name of each note of the scale and where it is on the fiddle.

Lesson 5
Repeat Signs

At the end of each line of the next tune there are two dots before the barline. This symbol :| means to repeat the music just played. It is called a repeat sign. The repeat sign at the end of the first line means to play again from the beginning.

At the beginning of the second line, there is a barline followed by two dots |: . This symbol marks the place a repeat is to begin. The repeat sign at the end of the second line means to repeat back to the symbol at the beginning of the second line.

Shortnin' Bread

Another type of repeat is the first and second ending. Notice the brackets over the measures at the end of the first line of "Oh, Susanna." The first time the line is played, the measure under the bracket with the "1" is played. This measure is called the first ending. It has a repeat sign, so a repeat is made. On the second playing, the measure under the first ending is skipped and the second ending, the measure under the bracket with the "2," is played.

Oh, Susanna

The first part of "Cindy" is the same as the first part of "Oh, Susanna," except for one note. Noticing similarities in tunes will help you memorize them faster. The second part of the tune uses the first and second fingers on the D string. First finger is E and second finger is F♯. They are notated on the bottom line and space.

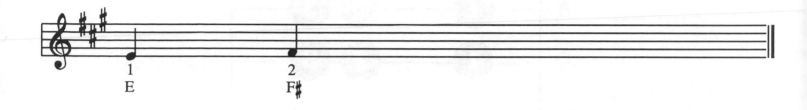

Cindy

Review

1. Play all of the tunes in Lessons 3–5 from memory. Go over any trouble spots.
2. Look at the music of these tunes and name each note by letter name. Refer to Lesson 4 if you need help.
3. Say the letter name of each note as you finger it on your fiddle.
4. Play the tunes again, giving special attention to left-hand position, bow position, clear tone, and being in tune. Watch your bow as you play.

Lesson 6
The D Scale

When two sharps are found at the beginning of the staff, the music is in the key of D. The sharps are F♯ and C♯. In this key the fingers are placed on the D and A strings like this diagram:

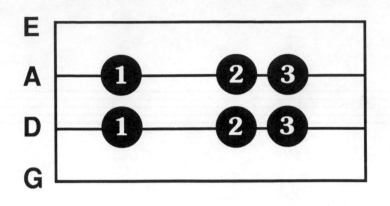

Play the following exercise starting on the D string, then place the first finger on the D string, then the second, followed by the third. After the third finger, go to the A string; then the first, second, and third fingers. Notice that the D scale is played the same way as the A scale, only starting on the D string.

Under each note you will see the finger number and the letter name of the note. These are to be memorized. Play slowly, concentrating on good tone and being in tune. Then practice the scale, saying the name of each note as it is played.

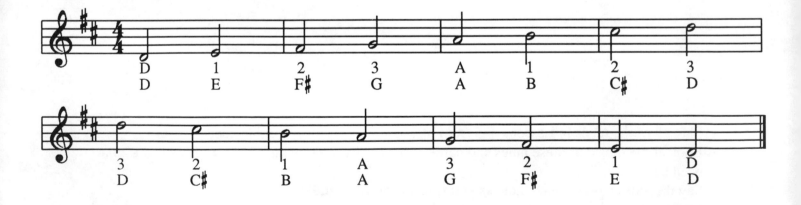

Dixie

Lesson 7
Time Signatures

The time signature is found at the beginning of the first line of a piece of music. The top number gives the number of beats per measure, and the bottom number tells what kind of note is equal to one beat.

All of the tunes we have learned so far have been in 4/4 or $\mathbf{C}$ common time. (The symbol $\mathbf{C}$ stands for common time and is another way of writing 4/4.) The top number tells us that there are four beats per measure, and the bottom number tells us the quarter note is equal to one beat. Here are some typical time signatures:

4 four beats per measure   **3** three beats per measure   **2** two beats per measure
4 quarter note = one beat   **4** quarter note = one beat   **4** quarter note = one beat

It is also possible for the eighth note or the half note to be equal to one beat. Here are some examples:

6 six beats per measure   **9** nine beats per measure   **12** twelve beats per measure
8 eighth note = one beat   **8** eighth note = one beat   **8** eighth note = one beat

4 four beats per measure   **3** three beats per measure   **2** two beats per measure
2 half note = one beat   **2** half note = one beat   **2** half note = one beat

Another symbol for 2/2 is $\mathbf{\phi}$. This is called cut time.

Pick-Up Notes

Sometimes the first measure of a tune does not have as many beats as the time signature calls for. These notes are called "pick-up" notes. The same number of beats as the first measure is taken from the last measure of the tune to make the total number of beats in all measures come out even.

Look at "Dixie," the tune you just learned. The first measure contains one beat, and the last measure contains three beats. These two incomplete measures combine to fill out a 4/4 measure. The next tune, "Wildwood Flower," is in 2/4. It begins with a one-beat pick-up and ends with a one-beat measure to fill out a 2/4 measure. The first tune in Lesson 8, "Soldier's Joy," also begins with a one-beat pick-up. In this case the extra beat is not made up at the end since the second part of the tune has an even number of beats.

Rests

At the beginning of the second and third lines of "Wildwood Flower" there is a symbol that is called a quarter rest. It means to be silent, or rest, for one beat. There is a rest equal to each kind of note.

Check Point - Types of Rests

1. Eighth rest   **7**   = one half beat.
2. Quarter test   **{**   = one beat.
3. Half rest   **▬**   = two beats.
4. Whole rest   **▬**   = four beats.

18

Wildwood Flower

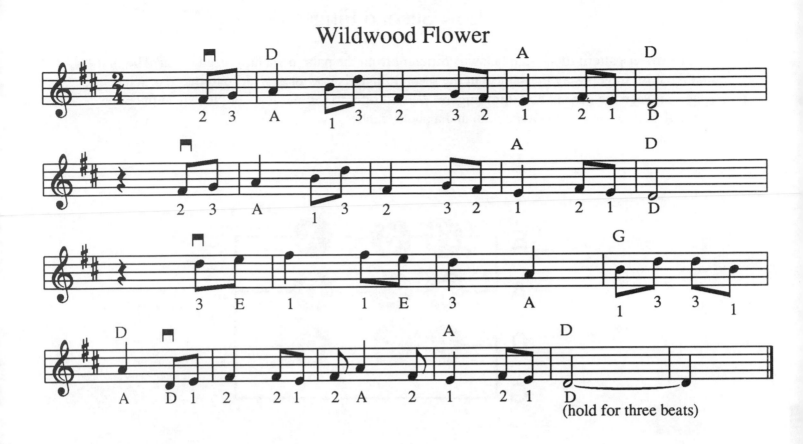

This tune is written in cut time ¢ . There are two beats per measure, and the half note is equal to one beat. The quarter notes get one half beat each.

Angeline the Baker

Lesson 8
Low Second Finger

The finger pattern illustrated below is different from the pattern we have used so far. The first and the third fingers stay the same, but the second finger is now played close to the first, with space between the second and third fingers. We will refer to this as "low" or "lo" since the pitch is a half step lower. Here is a diagram and a photograph:

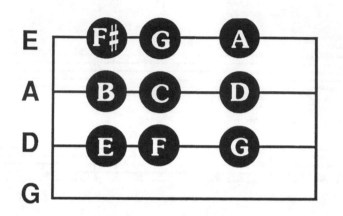

Photo by Charmaine Lanham

Notice that the second finger on the E string is noting a G instead of a G♯. This finger pattern is used on the A string when a C♮ (natural) is needed instead of C♯. It is also used on the D string when an F♮ (natural) is needed instead of an F♯.

The second part of "Soldier's Joy" has five G naturals, or low second fingers, on the D string. Be certain to keep the second finger back against the first finger and leave enough space between the second and third fingers. Watch out for the second fingers on the A string and remember to play them high enough.

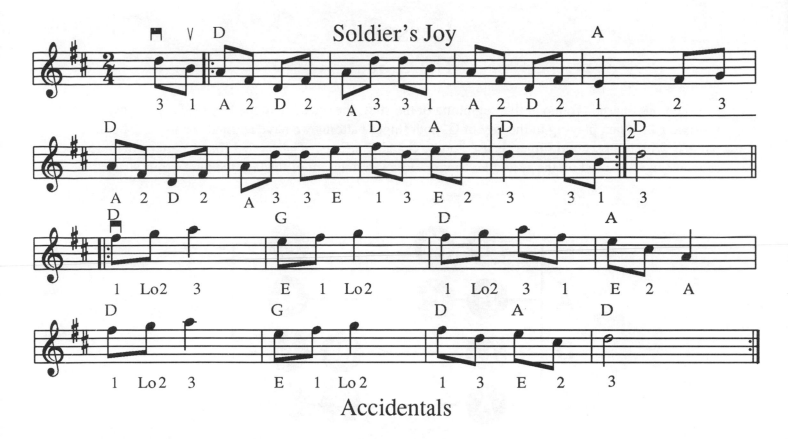

Soldier's Joy

Accidentals

Sometimes the note needed in a tune is not in the key of the tune. When this happens, an accidental is used. Accidentals can be sharps ♯, flats ♭, or naturals ♮. They are always written before the note and are good for all similar notes in that measure. For example, look at the third measure of the third line of "Going to Boston." The natural sign means both of the C's in that measure are natural (low). However, another natural sign is needed in the next measure to make that C♯ a C♮.

Check Point - Accidentals

1. Sharps ♯ raise a pitch one half step.
2. Flats ♭ lower a pitch one half step.
3. Naturals ♮ negate a sharp or flat (sharps are lowered, flats are raised).

Going to Boston

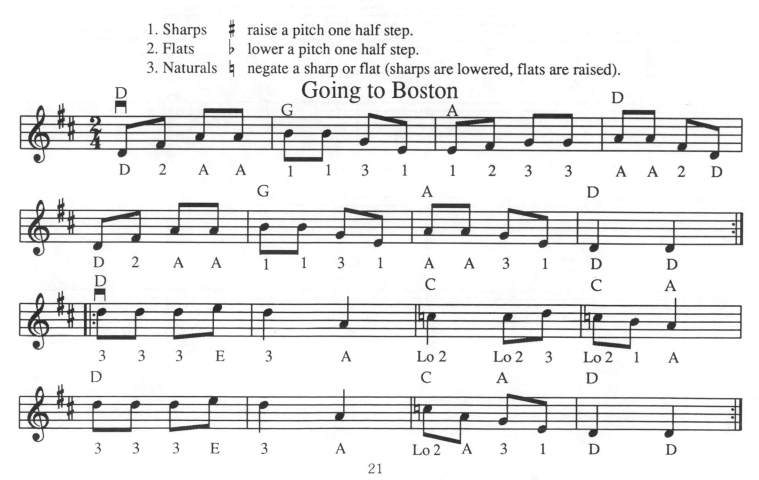

Lesson 9
The G Scale

When one sharp is found at the beginning of the staff, the music is in the key of G. The only sharp is F#. When playing in the key of G, both finger patterns we have learned are used. The first pattern, with high second finger, is used on he G and D strings. The second finger pattern, with low second finger, is used on the A and E strings. Here is a diagram of the G scale on all four strings:

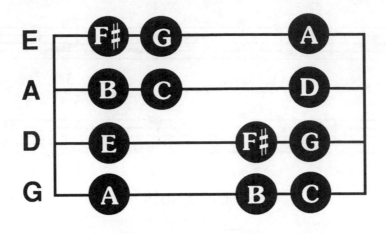

The following exercise is a two-octave G scale. The finger number and the letter name of each note are written beneath the note. Practice the scale slowly, memorizing the name of each note as you play.

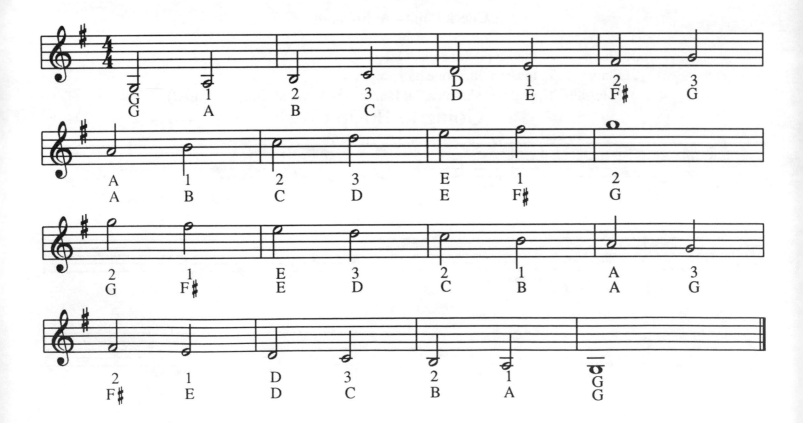

This arrangement of "Flop Eared Mule" outlines the basic melody of the tune. It should be played in the middle of the bow, concentrating on a clean, full sound. Make certain to observe the repeat sign each time the tune is played.

Flop Eared Mule

Review

1. Play all of the tunes in Lessons 3–8 from memory.
2. Play "Liza Jane" (Lesson 3) in the key of D by starting with second finger on the D string. Play it in the key of G by starting with second finger on the G string.
3. Play "Camptown Races" (Lesson 3) in D by starting on the A string. Play it in G by starting on the D string.
4. Play "Buffalo Gals" (Lesson 4) in D by starting on the D string. Play it in G by starting on the G string.
5. Play "Shortnin' Bread" and "Oh, Susanna" (Lesson 5) in D by starting on the D string. Play the tunes in G by starting on the G string.
6. Practice the A, D, and G scales, naming the notes by letter as you play.

Lesson 10

This tune is an American folk song that was used as a "play party" tune. Be very careful to play the second finger on the D string high and the second finger on the A string low.

Skip to My Lou

This tune is of Irish origin, but has been played so often in traditional American circles that it is also thought of as an American tune. Make certain to keep the low second fingers in tune. Be careful on each string crossing to touch only the string you mean to play.

The Girl I Left Behind Me

Lesson 11
The Fourth Finger

When the fourth finger is placed on the string, it should note the same pitch as the next higher open string. In other words, the fourth finger on the A should sound the same as open E, the fourth finger on the D the same as open A, and the fourth finger on the G the same as open D. The fourth finger is often used to make the bowing smoother by eliminating string changes or string crossings. Here are a diagram and photograph of fourth-finger placement:

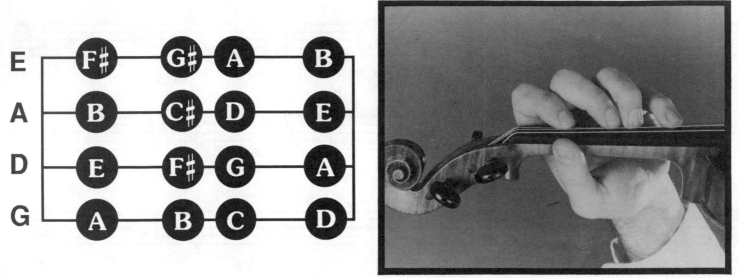

Photo by Charmaine Lanham

Practice this exercise to build strength in your fourth finger. After you learn it on the A string, practice it on the E, D, and G strings.

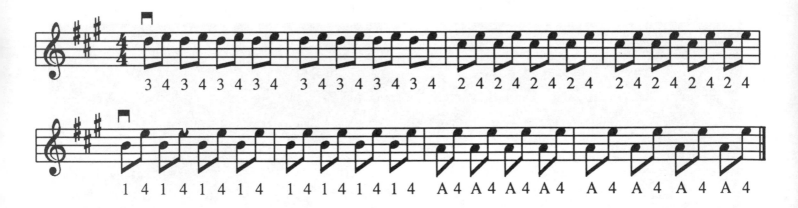

The Shuffle

Fiddlers often use a bowing pattern known as a shuffle. The shuffle is a long bow stroke followed by two short bow strokes, with the long stroke being exactly twice as long as each short stroke. This rhythm is repeated over and over. It is often written as a quarter note followed by two eighth notes. The next several tunes use this type of bowing. Practice slowly at first and gradually build up speed. The shuffle is used to perform a rhythmic style of fiddling great for square dancing.

Bile Them Cabbage Down

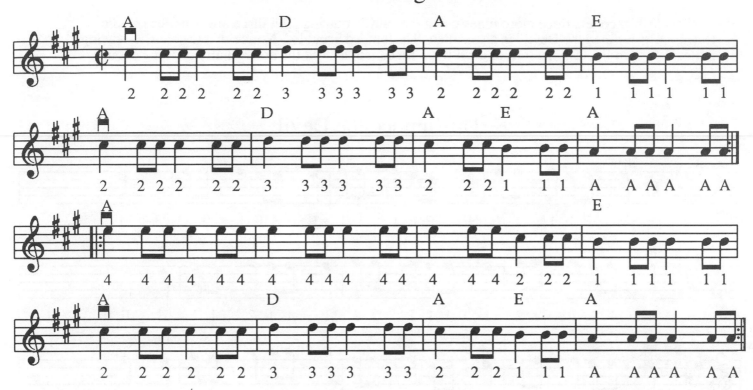

Old Joe Clark

Lesson 12

This lesson covers three more tunes using the shuffle bowing. All three are American fiddle tunes. "Up Jumped the Devil" is also called "Up Jumped Trouble." Notice that the shuffle-bowing pattern stops in the last measure of each line. Be certain to hold the dotted half note long enough.

Up Jumped the Devil

This arrangement of "Cripple Creek" presents the very basic melody in a shuffle-bowing style. Concentrate on making the string crossings even, with only one string sounding at a time.

Cripple Creek

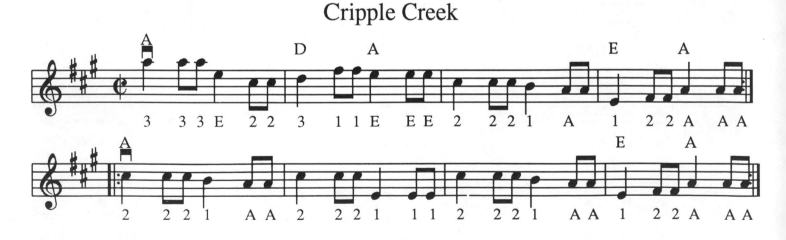

"Flop Eared Mule" is the same tune you learned in Lesson 9. The shuffle bowing remains steady throughout this arrangement. Notice the fourth fingers marked in the third and fourth lines of the tune. Make yourself learn the tune using the fourth finger. This will make the bowing sound smoother and increase the strength of the fourth finger.

Flop Eared Mule

Lesson 13
Double Stops

Fiddlers often play two strings at the same time. This is referred to as using double stops. The bow should be placed equally on both strings so that a good tone is produced on each string.

A very common type of double stop is sounded by playing an open string along with the string that is being noted. This technique is used in these arrangements of "Bile Them Cabbage Down" and "Old Joe Clark."

On "Bile Them Cabbage Down," the open E string is played with the melody on the A string. In the second measure, the first finger must be placed on the E string to sound the correct chord. Notice in the third line that the fourth finger and the open E string are played together on the same pitch. This is a very common type of double stop used in fiddling.

Bile Them Cabbage Down

MAJOR/MINOR

major
scale
pattern: WWHWWWH

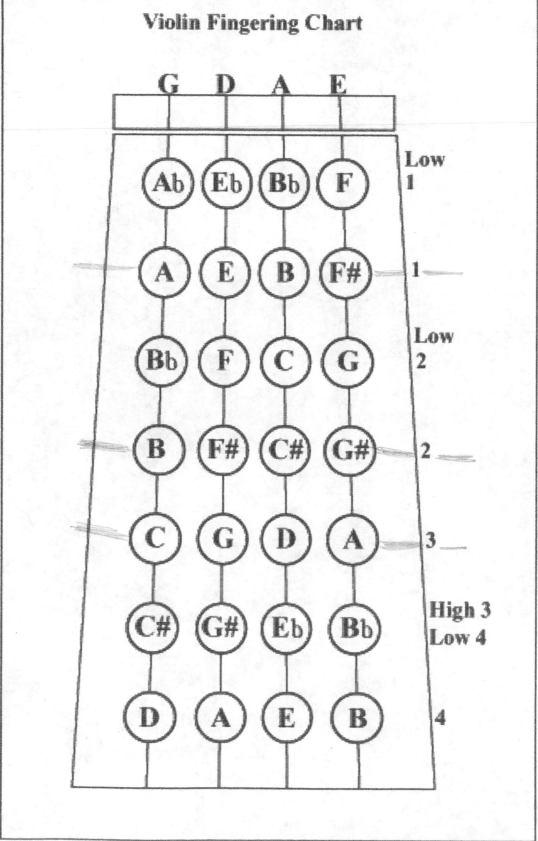

Violin Fingering Chart

Danny Boy

Feb 11

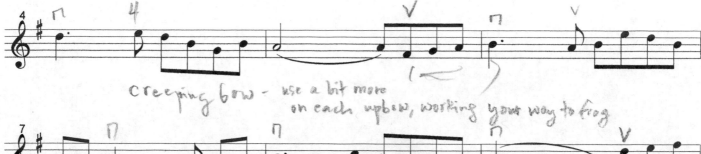

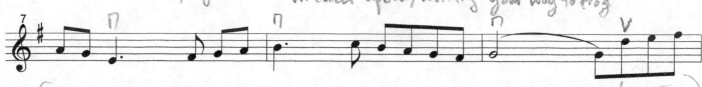

creeping bow - use a bit more
on each upbow, working your way to frog

frog

frog

OPEN STRINGS
AND THEIR
LETTER NAMES

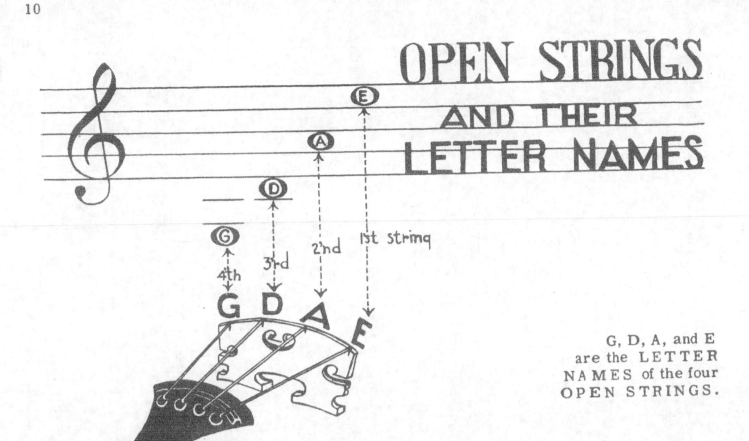

G, D, A, and E
are the LETTER
NAMES of the four
OPEN STRINGS.

Occasionally the OPEN STRINGS are given NUMBER NAMES
from the highest to the lowest (1st, 2nd, 3rd, and 4th strings) as shown
in the illustrations.

Draw a line from each OPEN STRING note to its LETTER NAME or
STRING NUMBER NAME on the bridge.

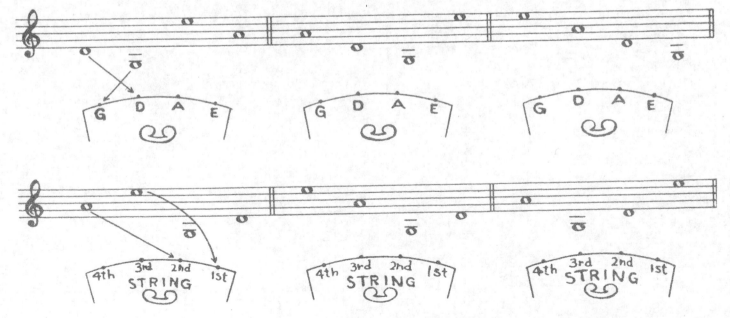

This arrangement of "Old Joe Clark" is played the same way as presented in Lesson 11, with the addition of an open string. In the fourth measure, the first finger has to be placed on the A string to play the proper chord. In the last measure of the third line, the first finger is placed on both the A and D strings. Whenever one finger notes two strings, more of the finger should touch the higher string than the lower to insure proper intonation. In this case, more of the first finger touches the A string than the D string.

Old Joe Clark

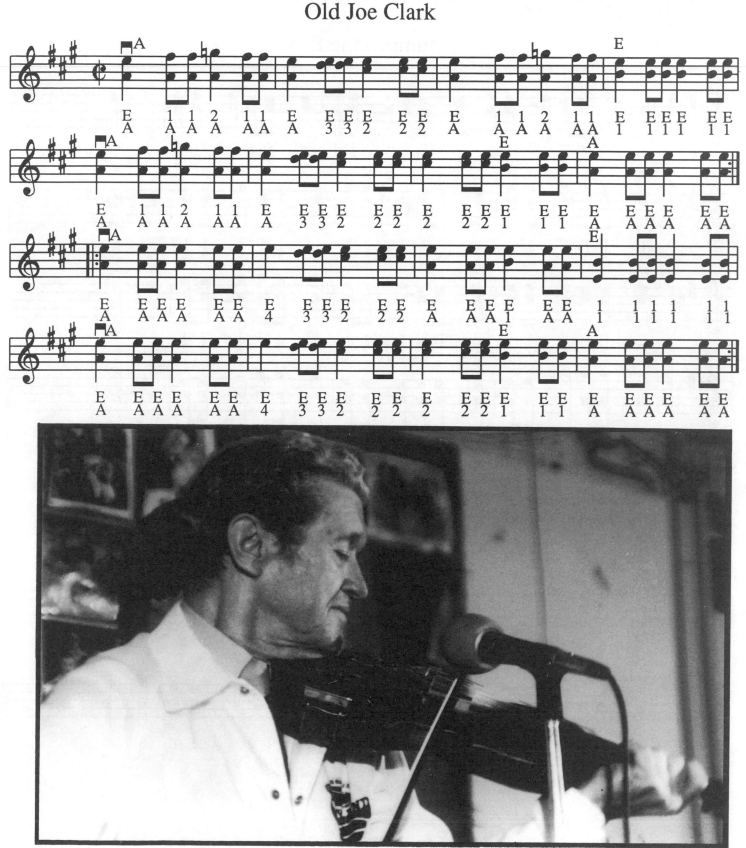

Lesson 14

As was discovered in Lesson 13, often double stops require noting both strings. Such is the case in this arrangement of "Up Jumped the Devil." When playing the second line, it is necessary to place the second finger on the E string as close as possible to the third finger on the A string. It should feel like the second finger is almost under the third.

Up Jumped the Devil

When using double stops, it is not necessary to play the entire tune with every note doubled. In fact, variety makes listening to fiddling more interesting. Another more practical reason not to play every note as a double stop is that some parts of a melody are easier to play clearly as single notes. Here are the last two lines of "Up Jumped the Devil" with some of the notes doubled and some of the notes played alone. Practice the tune with both possibilities to determine which works best for you.

This arrangement combines shuffle bowing using double stops and single notes on a tune first presented in Lesson 8. In measures one and five the A string is played alone. However, in measures four and seven it is to be doubled with the fourth finger on the D string. Notice that the shuffle bowing is not continuous, but allows the rhythm of the melody to come through.

Going to Boston

Tommy Williams

33

Lesson 15

The symbols ⌢ and ⌣ mean to play the notes they connect with one bow stroke. In other words, when two notes are connected by a ⌢ and the bow is going down, both of the notes are played down bow. Likewise, when the bow is going up, both of the notes are played up bow.

When the notes are different, the left fingers change while the bow goes the same direction. This is called a slur. When the notes are the same, the values of the notes are added. For example, a half note tied to a quarter note is held for 2 + 1 or 3 beats. This is called a tie.

In the next few tunes, the slur is used to keep the shuffle bowing constant, even though the pitches change. Notice the first two lines of "Mississippi Sawyer." Slurs are occasionally added so that the bowing pattern remains ♩ ♪ ♪ ♩ ♪ ♪ even though the pitches change more frequently. Keep the feel of the shuffle alive as you play this tune.

Mississippi Sawyer

Slurs are used in this tune to keep the shuffle bowing pattern alive. Notice that each measure starts down bow.

Soldier's Joy

Chubby Wise

Lesson 16

Once again we have another version of "Flop Eared Mule." This arrangement uses shuffle bowing with slurs to embellish the melody. By adding notes around the basic melody and keeping the shuffle bowing constant, a real sense of "fiddling" is felt. This tune is often played in the key of D. This is accomplished by starting on first finger on the E string (instead of on the A string) and playing every note one string higher.

Flop Eared Mule

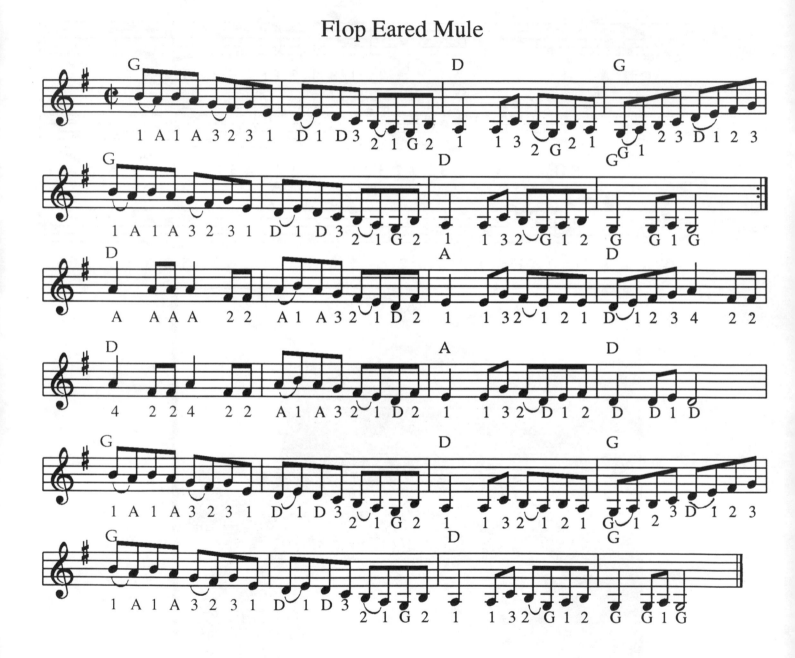

Shuffle bowing and notes added around the melody make this version of "Skip to My Lou" sound more like "fiddling" than the unadorned melody found in Lesson 10. Remember that the second finger is high on the D string and low on the A string.

Skip to My Lou

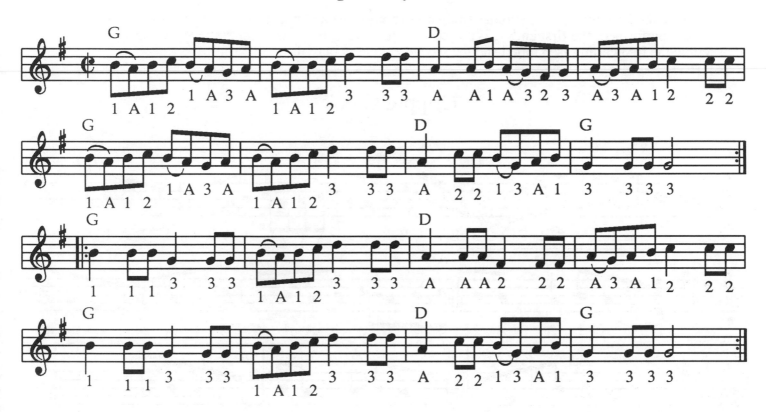

Review

1. Create a "theme-and-variations" arrangement of "Flop Eared Mule" by playing the tune the way you learned it in Lesson 9 followed by the way you learned it in Lesson 12 followed by the way you learned it in Lesson 16.

2. Create a "theme-and-variations" arrangement of "Skip to My Lou" by playing the tune the way you learned it in Lesson 10 followed by the way you learned it in Lesson 16.

Lesson 17

Slurs are used in this arrangement of "Cripple Creek" to keep the shuffle bowing steady. This gives the tune a smoother feel than changing the bow on every note. It also gives a rhythmic drive good for square dancing.

Notice the first and second endings (measures four to five and nine to ten). The first time the music is performed, the first ending is played (measures four and nine). On the repeat of each section, the first ending is skipped and the second ending is played.

Cripple Creek

Once again notes are added around the basic melody of this tune to create a "fiddling" version. The shuffle bowing continues throughout the tune.

This is an "old-time" arrangement of "Old Joe Clark." In this version the melody goes to first finger E on the D string in the last measure of the third line. The accompaniment plays an E chord along with this measure. Another popular way to play the tune is to use a third-finger G on the D string in this measure. In this case, the accompaniment plays a G chord. See *Mel Bay's Deluxe Fiddling Method* pages 26–27 for the contrasting version.

Old Joe Clark

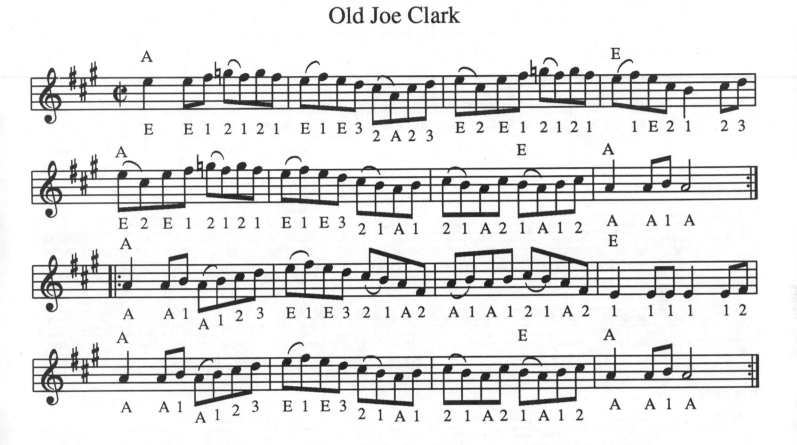

Review

1. Create a "theme-and-variations" arrangement of "Cripple Creek" by playing the tune the way you learned it in Lesson 12 followed by the way you learned it in Lesson 17.

2. Create a "theme-and-variations" arrangement of "Old Joe Clark" by playing the tune the way you learned it in Lesson 11 followed by the way you learned it in Lesson 13 followed by the way you learned it in Lesson 17.

Lesson 18
Introductions

The most common introduction to a fiddle tune is a four-beat shuffle on the key note. This has been referred to as "four taters," since it sounds rhythmically like "one tater-two tater-three tater-four tater." Often the introduction, or kick-off, will be "eight taters," or eight beats long. A common variation of the intro is to play a double stop consisting of the key note and another note in that chord. Here are examples in the keys of A, D, and G.

When a tune begins with pick-up notes, these notes are substituted for the last part of the introduction. The following examples show how this works with "The Girl I Left Behind Me" (Lesson 10) and "Soldier's Joy" (Lesson 15).

The Girl I Left Behind Me   **Soldier's Joy**

"Arkansas Traveler" is one of the most familiar American fiddle tunes. This arrangement begins with an introduction of "eight taters." Notice there are no guitar chords written over the introduction. Introductions are usually played solo, giving the fiddler the opportunity to set the tempo or speed of the tune. The actual tune starts in measure five. Keep the bowing steady, with the shuffle remaining constant throughout the tune.

Arkansas Traveler

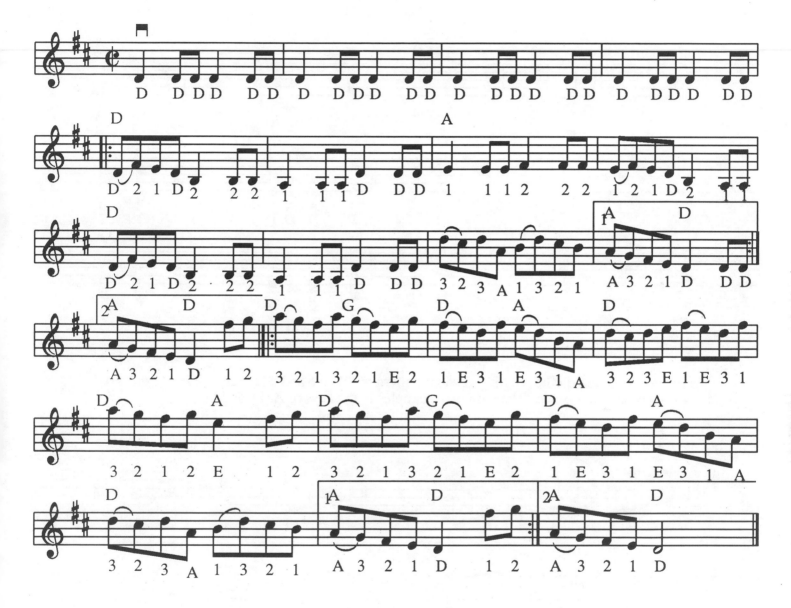

Lesson 19
Endings or Tags

At the end of a tune, fiddlers often play a tag to let the other musicians or dancers know that the tune is over. One of the most common tags is "Shave and a Haircut." By beginning on different strings, the same fingerings can be used to play "Shave and a Haircut" in the keys of A, D, and G.

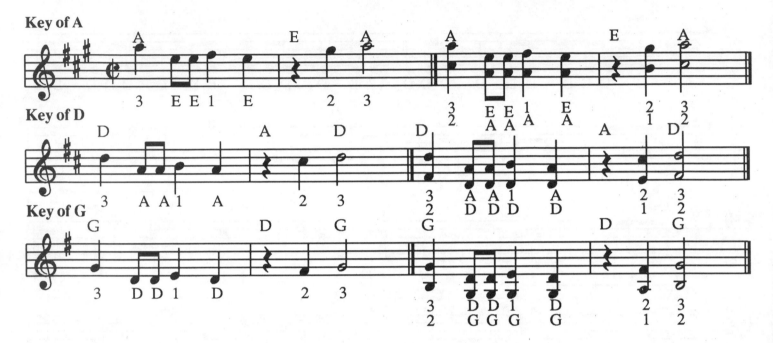

Many tags are based on the length and chord pattern of "Shave and a Haircut." One of the most common is a descending scale. Here are two examples in the keys of A, D, and G.

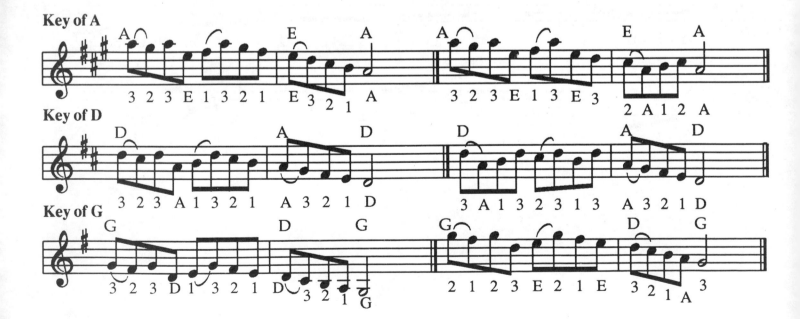

Two endings are often combined to make one longer ending. This has been called a "double tag" or a "double 'Shave and a Haircut.'" When a double tag is used, the notes usually keep moving at the end of the first tag so that the ending has a continuous flow. The first of the following examples combines some of the tags from the previous page. Then later examples show how tags may be connected to form a continuous double tag.

Learn these endings and experiment with creating endings of your own. The ideas presented here can be interchanged to form different endings. For additional ideas, see *Mel Bay's Fiddling Handbook* pages 59–61.

Lesson 20
Putting It All Together - Performance Time

In Lessons 3–18 we studied 21 fiddle tunes. In Lessons 18 and 19 we learned introductions and tags. Now it is time to put these together to create performances of the tunes.

1. "Liza Jane," "Camptown Races," "Buffalo Gals," and "Shortnin' Bread" (from Lessons 3, 4, and 5) are all in the key of A. Start each of these tunes with a "four-taters" introduction in the key of A as described in Lesson 18. Play the tune several times (at least three) and add a double tag in the key of A as described in Lesson 19.

2. "Oh, Susanna" and "Cindy" (Lesson 5) are also in the key of A, but begin with two pick-up notes. Start each of these tunes with a "four-taters" introduction, leaving off the last "tater." In other words, play "one-tater, two-tater, three-tater, four," then play the pick-up notes. After playing each tune through several times, add a double tag in the key of A as described in Lesson 19.

3. "Dixie" and "Wildwood Flower" (Lessons 6 and 7) are not usually performed with an introduction or a tag. Play through the tunes several times and end them by holding out the last note.

4. "Angeline the Baker," "Soldier's Joy," and "Going to Boston" (Lessons 7 and 8) are in the key of D. Start "Angeline the Baker" with a "four-taters" introduction in the key of D, play the tune several times, and add a double tag in the key of D. Start "Soldier's Joy" with the "four taters," allowing for the two pick-ups as you did with "Oh, Susanna" and "Cindy." Play the versions of the tune from Lessons 8 and 15 without pausing, and end with a double tag in the key of D. Start "Going to Boston" with "four taters" in the key of D, play the versions found in Lessons 8 and 14 several times, and end the tune with a double tag in the key of D.

5. "Flop Eared Mule," "Skip to My Lou," and "The Girl I Left Behind Me" (Lessons 9 and 10) are in the key of G. Each tune begins with a "four- (or eight-) tater" introduction. Play "Flop Eared Mule" as found in Lessons 9, 12, and 16 followed by a double tag in the key of G. Play "Skip to My Lou" as found in Lessons 10 and 16 followed by a double tag in G. Play "The Girl I Left Behind Me" several times, ending it with a double tag in G.

6. "Bile Them Cabbage Down," "Old Joe Clark," "Up Jumped the Devil," and "Cripple Creek" (Lessons 11 and 12) are in the key of A. Begin each tune with a "four- (or eight-) tater" introduction in A. Play "Bile Them Cabbage Down" as presented in Lessons 11 and 13 followed by a double tag in the key of A. Play "Old Joe Clark" as presented in Lessons 11, 13, and 17 followed by a double tag in the key of A. Play "Up Jumped the Devil" as presented in Lessons 12 and 14 followed by a double tag in A. Play "Cripple Creek" as presented in Lessons 12 and 17 followed by a double tag in A.

7. "Mississippi Sawyer" (Lesson 15) is in the key of D. Begin with a "four- (or eight-) tater" introduction, allowing for the pick-up notes to replace the last "tater." Play the tune several times and end with a double tag in the key of D.

8. "Arkansas Traveler" (Lesson 18) is in the key of D. Play the introduction as presented in Lesson 18. Then play the tune several times followed by a double tag in D.

Technique Review

It is always important to use correct positions when fiddling. Use of proper technique will make your playing sound better and make it more efficient. As you review the tunes you have learned, keep the following check points in mind.

Check Points

Fiddle Position
1. Keep fiddle up on shoulder.
2. Keep fiddle parallel to floor (scroll end as high as chinrest end).
3. Hold instrument up with chin and shoulder.

Left-Hand Position
1. Thumb straight, touching fiddle neck above the knuckle.
2. "Window" visible under neck between thumb and index finger.
3. "Egg" in palm to keep palm away from fiddle neck.
4. Left arm and elbow directly under fiddle.
5. Fingertips touch strings from above.

Bow-Hand Position
1. First finger touching bow between first and second joints.
2. Pinky curved with tip touching bow.
3. Middle and ring fingers wrapped comfortably.
4. All fingers curved, spread apart, and relaxed.
5. Thumb bent outward, tip on bow, forming a circle with fingers.

Bow Placement
1. Bow midway between bridge and fingerboard.
2. Keep bow straight (exactly perpendicular to strings).
3. Pull the bow with a steady stroke.
4. Most fiddle tunes should be played in the middle of the bow.

Practice the tunes you have learned in front of a mirror. Check your positions as you play, correcting them as needed. Concentrate on one thing at a time. For example, practice "Liza Jane" watching fiddle position. Then practice "Camptown Races" watching left-hand position. Review the tunes until you can play them comfortably with correct positions.

Lesson 21
Form

Form describes the basic structure or outline of the music. The following tune, "Rose Tree," begins with an eight-measure melody which ends at the first ending. This part of the tune is called the "A" section. The music is repeated, thus making the section and its repeat an AA form. There is a second section to the tune, which is called "B" because it is different from the A section. It is also repeated, giving the tune an overall form of AABB.

Most fiddle tunes have an AABB form; however, many other forms are possible. For example, "Flop Eared Mule" (Lessons 9, 12, 16) has an AABA form because the original theme is used to close the tune. It is possible for a tune to have many different parts, giving it a larger form, but most fiddle tunes have two parts which are repeated and varied. This type of form can also be considered "theme and variation." Understanding the overall form of a tune will make the tune easier to memorize and help you keep track of where you are in the tune when performing it.

Rose Tree

This tune also has an AABB form. Be certain to play the C♮ in the second line with a low second finger. The C♯ in the third line is played with a high second finger.

Over the Waterfall

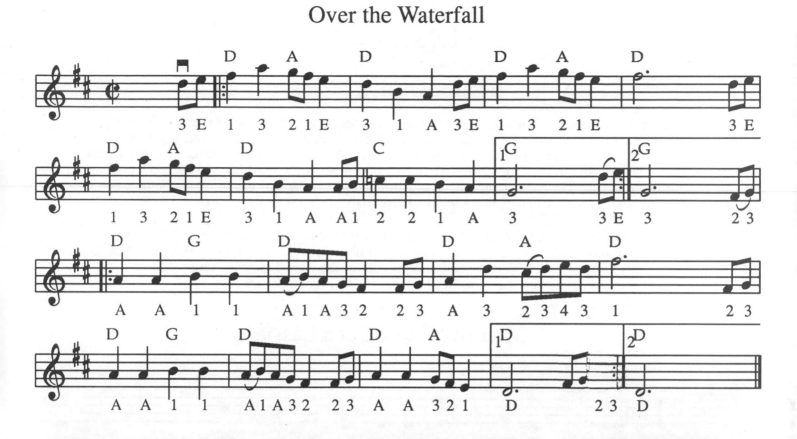

Bobby Hicks and Vassar Clements

Lesson 22

Dotted Quarter Notes

As you learned in Lesson 3, adding a dot to a half note increases the value of the note by half. The same is true for other note values. When a quarter note is equal to one beat, and is followed by a dot, it becomes a dotted quarter note equal to one and a half beats. When a quarter note is equal to one half of a beat, as in cut time, and is followed by a dot, it becomes a dotted quarter note equal to three fourths of a beat. The same relationship of a dot adding one half of the value of the note applies to any kind of note whether it is a whole, half, quarter, eighth or sixteenth.

This tune from the British Isles makes use of the dotted quarter followed by an eighth note several times in the second part. Count carefully as you play this section. In the last measure of the first line the E is to be played with a fourth finger instead of the open E string. This will avoid having to cross two strings with the bow thus making the bowing smoother.

My Love She's But a Lassie

This tune is also from the British Isles and makes use of the dotted-quarter/eighth rhythm. In the second measure, it is once again necessary to use the fourth finger instead of the open A to make the bowing smoother. Count carefully as you play.

Newcastle

Buddy Spicher

49

Lesson 23
Waltzes

In Lesson 7 we learned about time signatures. The time signature for a waltz is 3/4. This means there are three beats in each measure and the quarter note is equal to one beat. Waltzes should be played with a long, smooth bow stroke, using as much of the bow on each note as possible.

Southwind

This is a traditional Irish waltz with a very beautiful, simple melody. It begins with two pick-ups which are counted "3 &." The measures with the dotted quarter/eighth/quarter are counted "1, 2 & 3." In the third measure from the end, be certain to play the C with a low second finger on the A and the F♯ with a high second finger on the D string.

This is also an Irish waltz, attributed to Turlough O Carolan, a 17th century Irish harper. He used this melody, which was originally called "The Bonnie Cuckoo," and wrote words to it about a battle between the fairies of Sheebeg (the Little Fairy Hill) and the fairies of Sheemore (the Big Fairy Hill).

Like "Southwind," this tune begins with two pick-ups and is counted the same way. Observe the fingerings, as sometimes fourth fingers are used, and other times open strings are needed to make the bowing smoother. Keep the beat steady and use long bow strokes.

Si Bheag, Si Mhor (Sheebeg, Sheemore)

Lesson 24
The A Scale

The low octave of the A scale uses a different finger pattern than we have used so far.   In this scale, the third finger on the G and D strings is played high, a whole step above the second finger. The fourth finger is placed close to the third finger.   The intervals between fingers one, two, three, and four are now whole step, whole step, half step.   Here are a photo of the finger pattern on the G and D strings and a diagram of the two-octave A scale:

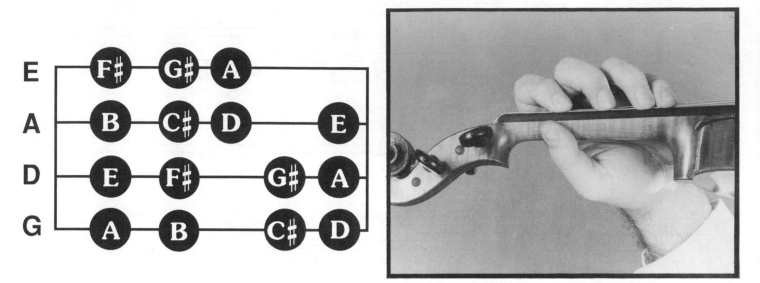

Photo by Charmaine Lanham

Practice the low-octave A scale slowly until you can play it in tune comfortably.   Memorize the way it feels to stretch the third finger.   Then practice the two-octave scale using the fourth fingers as indicated.

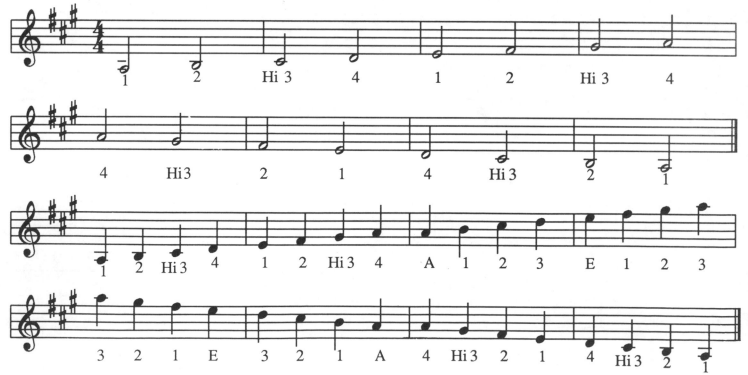

52

This is the first part of "Bile Them Cabbage Down" played one octave lower. Practice it carefully until you can play it in tune. Be certain to use the fourth fingers as marked. Then add this new variation to your arrangement of the tune.

Bile Them Cabbage Down

This tune is usually thought of as a "bluegrass" fiddle tune. It uses the shuffle bowing. There is a D♯ in the first measure which is played with high third finger or low fourth finger on the A string. It occurs again in the fifth measure. The other D's (third fingers) on the A string are natural and are played in the normal position. There are several fourth fingers indicated throughout the tune. Using these will make the bowing smoother and the tune easier to play fast.

The Sandy River

Lesson 25
Mixolydian Mode

Very often in fiddle music the seventh note of the scale is played a half step flat. The resulting scale is called the Mixolydian mode. In the key of A, the Mixolydian mode is A-B-C♯-D-E-F♯-G-A. Another typical characteristic of fiddle music is that it will switch back and forth between the normal seventh scale degree (major scale) and the flatted-seventh scale degree (Mixolydian mode). This "mixing of modes" takes place in the next two tunes. Watch carefully for G♯'s, being certain to play them high, and G♮'s, being certain to play them low.

This is an American tune which has been traced to Albemarle County, Virginia. The version here is based on a Pennsylvania fiddler's rendition. This rhyme goes with the tune:

> Fine times at our house, Sally's got a little one,
> A great big yellow devil just like the other one.

Be certain to play the third fingers on the G string high. All of the G's are natural, so the third finger on the D string and the second finger on the E string are played low.

Triplets are found in the second measure of the third and fourth lines. They are played by making each of the eighth notes equal in length, all sounded within the length of a quarter note (three eighth-note triplets = one quarter note).

Fine Times at Our House

This is an old-time bluegrass-style tune. It is often played as a guitar instrumental. The tune opens with the fourth finger on the D string and the open A sounding the same pitch. There is a constant trade-off between the modes (major scale and Mixolydian), so sometimes the third finger on the D string is high and sometimes it is not. The same is true for the second finger on the E string.

Salt River

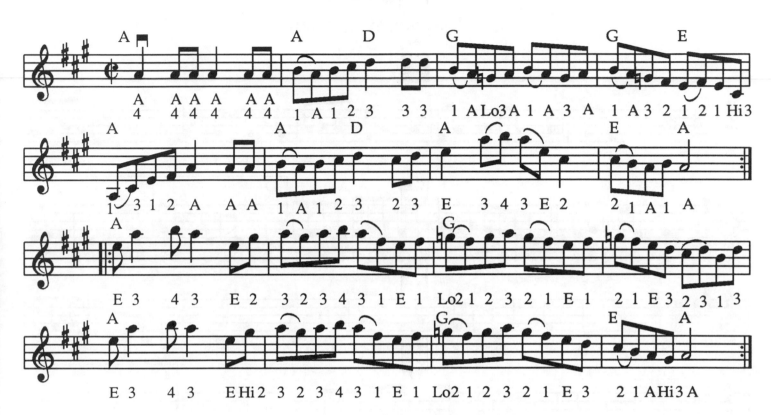

Lesson 26

Since the key of D has a C♯, its finger pattern on the G string has a high third finger. This arrangement of "Mississippi Sawyer" is one octave lower than the arrangement in Lesson 15. Be certain to observe the fourth finger and open A string markings as indicated.

Mississippi Sawyer

Tater Tate

This is one of many tunes that goes by more than one name. I learned the tune from two different sources, one person calling it "Chinky Pin," and the other calling it "Too Young to Marry." This is a rather straightforward arrangement. It should be played at a medium tempo with a good "bounce" to the tune.

Chinky Pin or Too Young to Marry

Lesson 27

This is one of the more popular fiddle tunes in country music, possibly because of the dance by the same name that is done to this tune. This version has an uneven form. Notice the first part is repeated, but the second is not. In fact, the last four measures of the second part are a variation on the first four measures of the part. The slurs in the tune do not follow the ordinary shuffle style. The pick-up notes are slurred into the downbeat of the first measure. This is an often-used characteristic of fiddle bowing.

A note for the accompanist: The chords indicated are correct. The fourth measure does *not* go to an E chord.

Cotton Eyed Joe

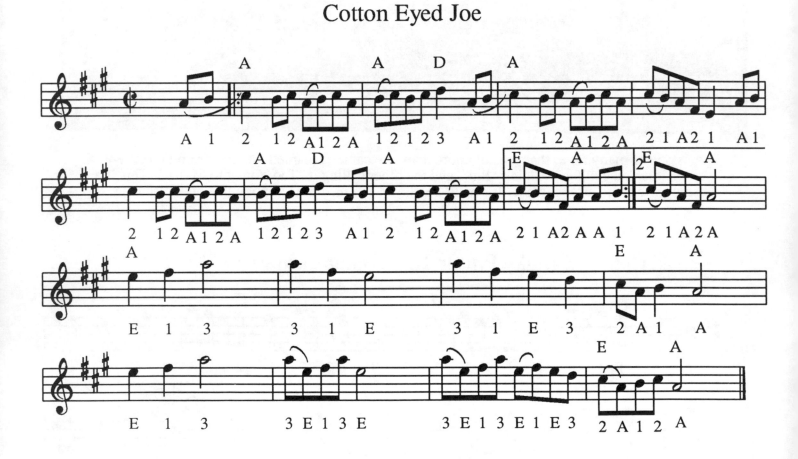

This is a slow Scottish tune based on an arrangement by J. Scott Skinner. There are many slurs, as the tune is imitating the constant sound of the bagpipes. Likewise, the accompaniment should stay on an A chord, leaving out the third. After you have learned the tune, try playing as much as possible of it bowing the A and E strings together as a drone. This is especially effective in the first two sections.

The small notes found throughout the tune are called "grace notes." They are to be played very quickly, right on the beat. Sometimes grace notes are played just ahead of the beat, depending on the style of music. Use your ear to determine what sounds best to you.

The Cameron Highlanders

Lesson 28
Dotted Eighth/Sixteenth

As we learned in earlier lessons, adding a dot to a note increases it by half. The eighth note is equal to one half of a beat, so when it is followed by a dot, it is equal to three fourths of a beat. That makes it three times longer than a sixteenth note. The following tunes make use of the dotted-eighth/sixteenth rhythm. Remember to give the dotted eighth three fourths of the beat and the sixteenth one fourth of the beat.

"Scotland the Brave" is a traditional Scottish tune, often played with the feeling of a march. Although the tune may be played in several keys, the arrangement here is in D so that the tune falls within a good vocal range. Here are the words that go with the tune. Note that the repeats in he music do not apply when the song is sung.

> Hark when the night is falling, Hear, hear, the pipes are calling.
> Loudly and proudly falling down through the glen.
> Now feel your heart a-beating, Now feel your spirits leaping,
> High as the spirits of the old Highland men.

Chorus
> Torn and gallant fame, Scotland, my mountain hame,
> High may your proud banners gloriously wave.
> Land of my high endeavor, Land of the shining river,
> Land of my heart forever, Scotland the Brave.

> Out by the misty highlands, Down by the purple islands,
> Brave are the hearts that beat beneath Scottish skies.
> Wild are the winds that meet you, Staunch are the friends that greet you,
> High as the love that shines in fair maiden's eye.

Scotland the Brave

This arrangement of "Harvest Home" incorporates several features of Scottish fiddling. First of all, the dotted-eighth/sixteenth rhythm is used throughout. Be certain to play the dotted eighth three fourths of a beat and the sixteenth one fourth. This is even more critical in this tune because of the triplets found in the last measure of the first and third lines. Scottish fiddling often uses triplets and dotted eighth/sixteenths in contrast within the same tune.

Another technique found in Scottish fiddling as well as in Irish and some Canadian fiddling is the use of the "snap-style" bowing found in the first two measures of the second part. This is a type of bowing ornament done by moving the bow very rapidly back and forth, using very little bow, at the beginning of a note. Learn the technique by starting slowly and building up speed. Use less than half an inch of bow for the fast notes.

Harvest Home

Lesson 29
Long Bow-Stroke Exercise

The tunes in this lesson require long bow strokes to produce a full tone. Practice playing long strokes on open strings while you watch your bow. Start the stroke all the way at the frog of the bow, going all the way to the tip. Reverse the stroke, coming completely back to the frog. Make certain the bow stays perfectly straight and rides on the string about one half of an inch from the bridge. Do this exercise 20 times (or more) on each string daily until it feels natural.

This beautiful waltz comes from Wales. It is to be played with long bow strokes to produce a full tone. The first section of the tune is repeated; however, the second is not.

Ash Grove

This is possibly the most popular of all hymn tunes. It is a Scottish melody which should be played with long bow strokes. Try to use the entire bow.

A very common fiddle ornamentation is used in the last two measures of the second line. The D (third finger) on the A string should be held for these two measures. In playing a long note such as this, fiddlers often slur to the note above as they finish a bow stroke before repeating the same note. This allows you to use two bow strokes to play one long (or tied) note. Notice that the bow should slur from the long note to the note above and change direction on the repeat of the long note. This keeps the emphasis on the note which is held, in this case the D.

Amazing Grace

Lesson 30

This tune is one of the most played tunes by fiddlers throughout North America. It appears under many titles including "Miss McLeod's Reel" (and various misspellings), "Hop Light Ladies," "Did You Ever See the Devil, Uncle Joe," and "Uncle Joe." It is considered to be both an Irish and a Scottish tune.

One interesting characteristic of this tune is that both parts end on a D chord instead of the tonic chord, G. When repeating the tune, do not play the measure marked "Last Time Only." This measure acts as a coda (ending) to the tune and should be played only at the very end.

Miss McLeod's Reel

This is another popular British Isles tune often played in the United States. It should be played at a medium tempo. Notice the three notes slurred together in the second, sixth, and seventh measures. Fiddlers often use this type of slurring when three notes fall together after a string crossing. The repeated A's in the last two measures of the third line are marked to be played with a fourth finger on the first one and an open A on the second. This is a common fiddling device that gives the music a feeling of moving on even though the note is repeated.

Swinging on a Gate

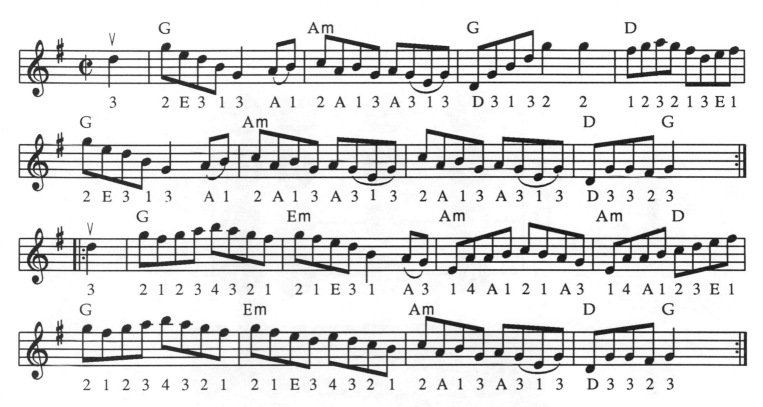

Lesson 31
Low First Finger and Low Fourth Finger

In all of the tunes we have learned so far, the first finger is placed about an inch from the nut (end of the fingerboard). When playing in other keys it is sometimes necessary to use a "low" first finger, placing it very close to the nut. The first finger usually notes an F♯ on the E string. Playing the finger low gives an F. On the A string the low first finger notes a B♭, on the D string an E♭, and on the G string an A♭. When noting a low first finger, there is a half step between the open string and the first finger, and a whole step between the low first and low second fingers.

The fourth finger can also be played "low," noting a half step above the third finger. Low fourth finger on the E string is B♭, on the A string is E♭, on the D string is A♭, and on the G string is D♭. Here is a diagram of these notes and positions:

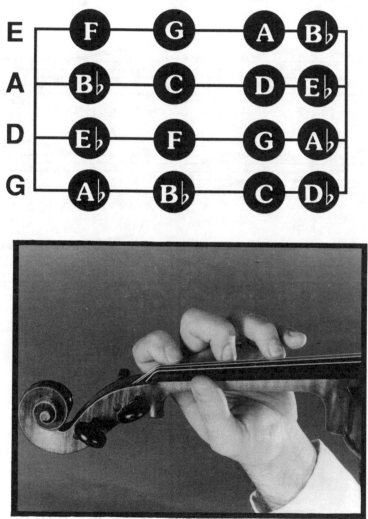

Photo by Charmaine Lanham

"Fisher's Hornpipe" is a popular tune among all styles of fiddlers. The tune is often played in the key of D and occasionally in G. This arrangement is in the original key of F. In F the first and fourth fingers are played low on the E string, and the first finger is played low on the A string. The first finger is high on the D and G strings. Practice slowly until these new finger patterns are comfortable. Remember there is a whole step between the first and second fingers and between the second and third fingers on the A and E strings.

Fisher's Hornpipe

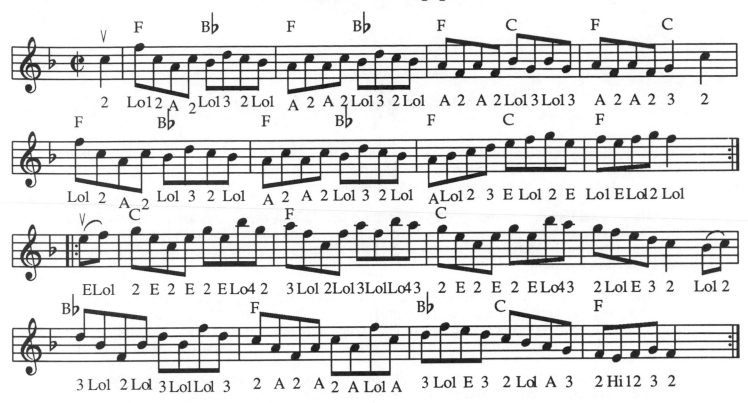

This tune is played in the key of D, so the finger patterns are the same as in earlier lessons. However, the third and fourth measures of the third line go to a B♭ chord. This means you have to use low first finger on the A and E strings and low fourth finger on the E string. Be certain to use high first and second fingers on the triplet in the last beat of the line. Another interesting characteristic of the tune is the short chromatic (half-step) scale found in the second measure of the third and fourth lines. This is done by playing third finger followed by high second, then sliding the finger back to low second. Try to move the finger so that the slide is not heard.

Snowflake Reel

67

Lesson 32
Understanding Keys and Scales

It is very important to know the key in which you are playing and how to play that scale. In written music, the key is determined by the number of sharps or flats. The sharps and flats dictate where the fingers are placed on each string. By learning the finger positions in each key and its scale, you will know where to place your fingers before you begin playing a tune.

The following scales are accompanied by diagrams showing how the fingers are placed on the strings. The diagrams show the finger patterns for all notes in first postion for each key. The written scales start and end on the note which is the name of the scale, so all of the notes on the diagram may not be used in practicing the scale.

Take note of the key signature (the sharps and flats) so you will recognize the key. Practice the scales slowly, concentrating on being exactly in tune. Each of these scales should be memorized. Both the fourth finger and the open string should be practiced in the scales. They are interchangable unless there is a flat or sharp for the pitch. In these exceptions the fourth finger is marked Hi or Lo.

This lesson should act as a reference in learning these few basic keys and scales. For a thorough source on keys, scales, fingerings, and chords, see *Mel Bay's Fiddling Handbook*.

Key of G - One Sharp

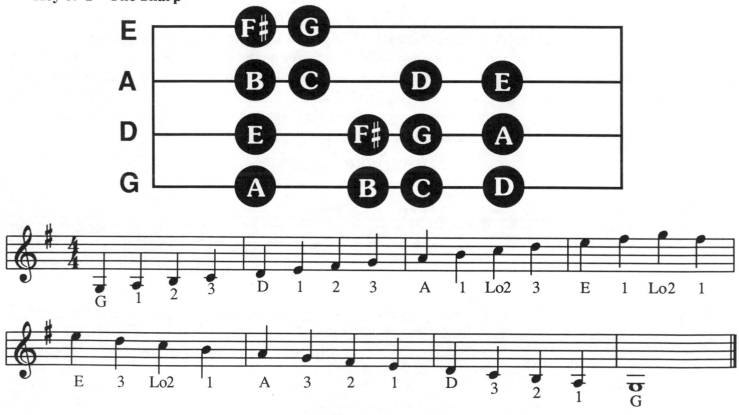

Key of A - Three Sharps

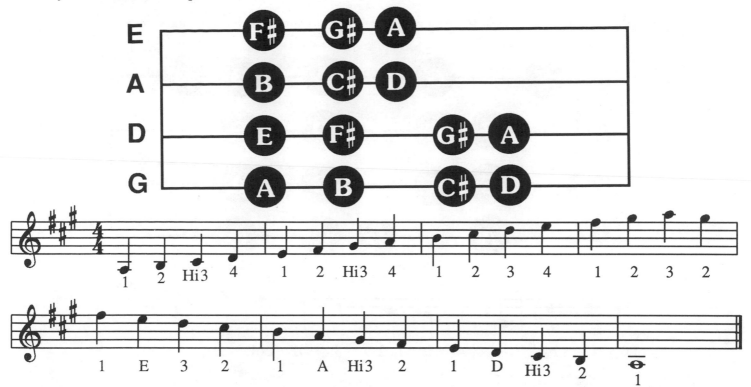

Key of B Flat - Two Flats

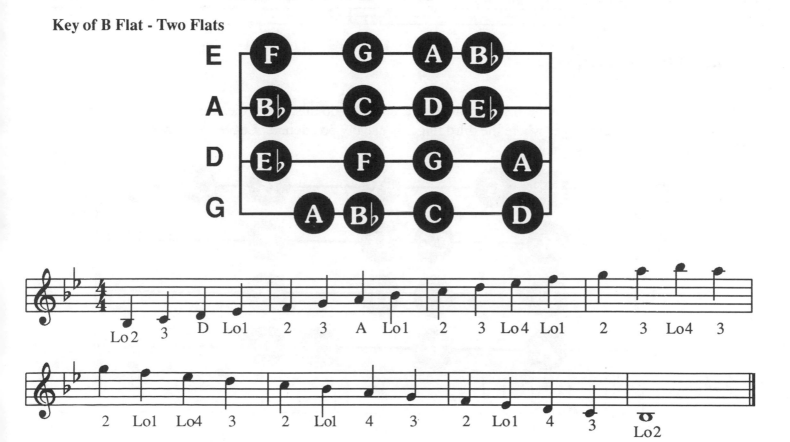

Key of C - No Flats or Sharps

In playing the C scale on the E string, the fourth finger can be stretched or extended to reach the high C.

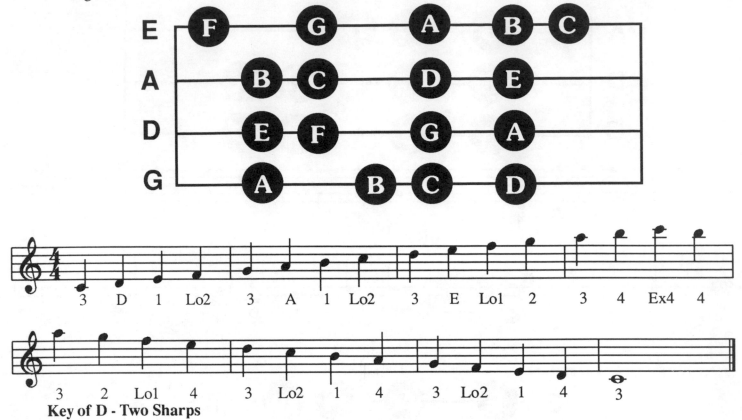

Key of D - Two Sharps

Play the D scale on the E string involves a shift. To do this, move the entire hand up the string, placing the first finger where the third finger is usually positioned. Leave the fingers on the string as you go up the scale.

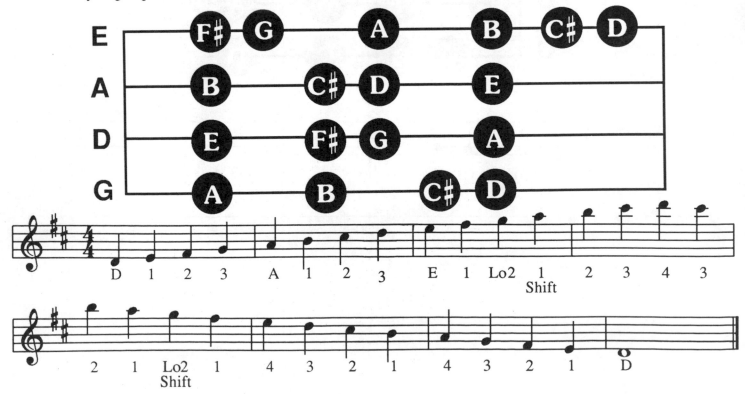

70

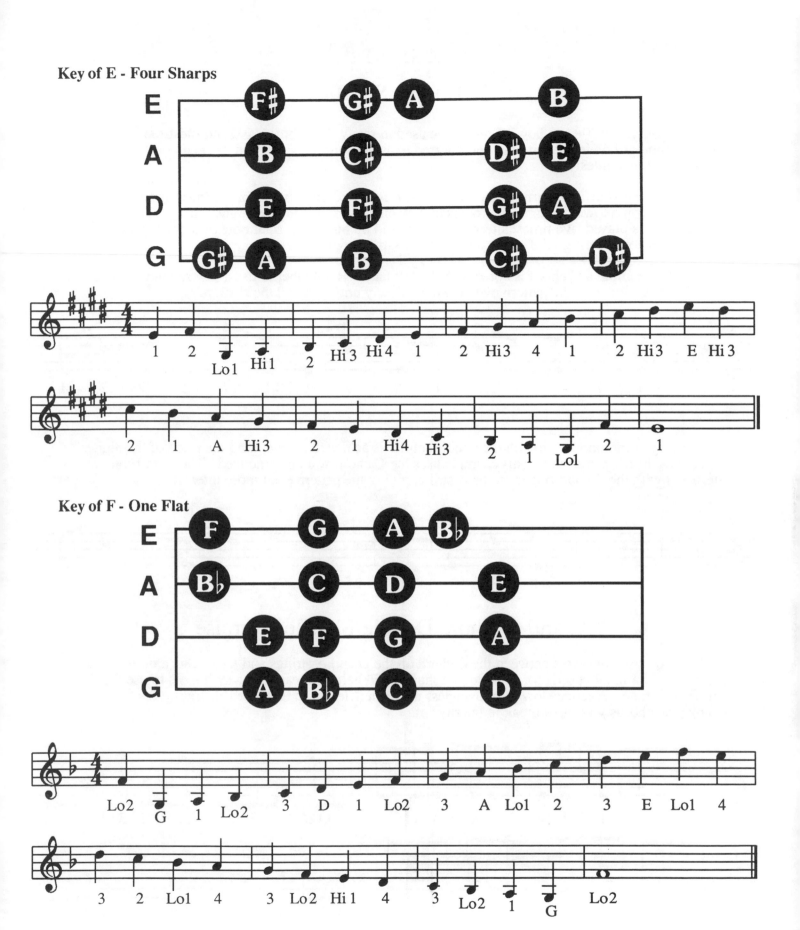

Lesson 33

Double Shuffle

The double shuffle is a bowing technique used in many show, bluegrass, and old-time tunes. It is such a popular bowing that it has been referred to as "Hokum bowing" and has been outlawed in many fiddling contests.

The double-shuffle pattern is 16 notes long and is played on two or more strings. It begins with two strokes on a lower string then crosses to play one stroke on the next higher string. This group of three notes is played five times, alternating down and up bow. The final note of the pattern is an up bow on the lower string. All of the notes are the same length.

In this example a C chord is noted with the left hand. Remember to use a low second finger on the A string. Practice the pattern over and over slowly until you feel the rhythm.

One very common variation on the double shuffle is achieved by changing the pitch of the higher string at each string crossing. This example uses the C chord you just practiced. The third finger is alternated with the second finger on the A string, giving the pattern even more interest.

C and G Chord Double-Shuffle Exercise

This exercise alternates between the C chord on the D and A strings and the G chord on the A and E strings. Changing chords for each double shuffle will help you learn the way it feels to use the shuffle in a tune. Practice slowly for evenness in the shuffle and in the chord changes. Try to change the chords without a break in the rhythm.

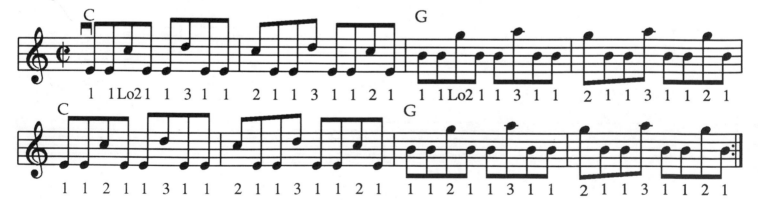

This tune is in the key of C (no flats or sharps); therefore, all of the second fingers, except on the G string, are low. It is played with a "bluesy" feel, using slides on the fourth fingers. Be careful not to overuse the slides, or the tune will sound even more "corny" than it already is. One slide which should be noted is in the third measure of the second line. The fourth finger is played low on the E string on a B♭ and slides down another half step to the A. The third finger must be moved out of the way. The second part of the tune is a double shuffle on the same chord structure as the first part.

Back Up and Push

73

Lesson 34

One of the most popular uses of the double shuffle is found in the tune "Orange Blossom Special." This exercise uses the chords found in the double-shuffle part of that tune. The first two lines are done on two strings. In the third and fourth lines, the same chords are used on three strings. When the second finger is used on the D string in the first two measures on the third line, it remains on the string through the set of three notes.

The same thing happens in the first two measures of the fourth line with the second finger on the A string. This is typical of the way the alternating pitch is used in the double shuffle. A full arrangement of "Orange Blossom Special" is found in the book *Advanced Fiddling* from Mel Bay Publications.

Orange Blossom Shuffle

This is an American fiddle tune, very similar to "Back Up and Push." This arrangement uses the double shuffle with the same chords which are used in "Orange Blossom."

Rubber Dolly

Lesson 35
Jigs

Jigs are played in 6/8 time. As you learned in Lesson 7, this means there are six beats in each measure and the eighth note is equal to one beat. When tunes written in 6/8 are played at a fast tempo, an accent falls on the first and fourth beats. This gives the feeling of two beats per measure, with each beat divided by three.

The tunes in Lessons 35 and 36 are all jigs, since they are in 6/8. A slip jig is a fiddle tune written in 9/8 played at a fast tempo. This gives the feeling of three beats per measure, with each beat divided by three.

One of the most familiar jigs is "Irish Washerwoman." All of the notes should be played very evenly. When playing the first two measures of the last line, the second-finger G on the E string should remain on the string as the other notes change. As a general rule, it is usually best to use the least amount of left-hand motion when fiddling.

Irish Washerwoman

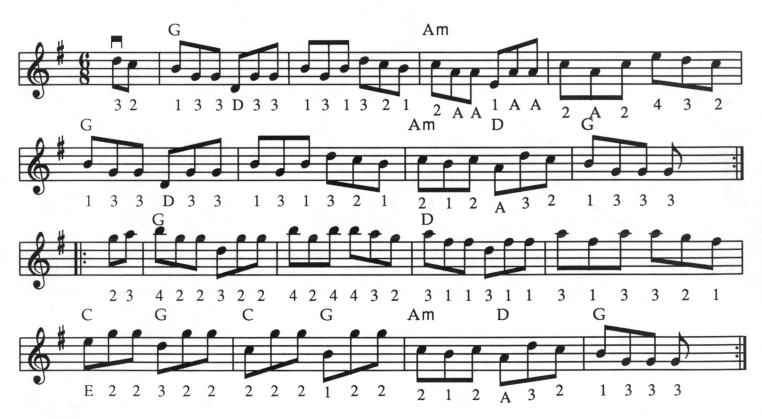

"Garry Owen" is an Irish tune printed under the name "Bundle and Go" in a collection by Aird in 1782. The tune was used by the U.S. Calvary for marching and was a favorite of General George Custer. This arrangement is in the key of G, although the tune is also played in the key of C. To transpose to C, play all of the notes on one string lower than written.

Garry Owen

This is an Irish-American tune. Remember to make the dotted eighths half again as long as the eighths. The fourth fingers should be used where indicated for smoother bowing. This tune sounds pretty as a slow jig. Try performing it slowly then speeding it up when you repeat the tune.

St. Patrick's Day

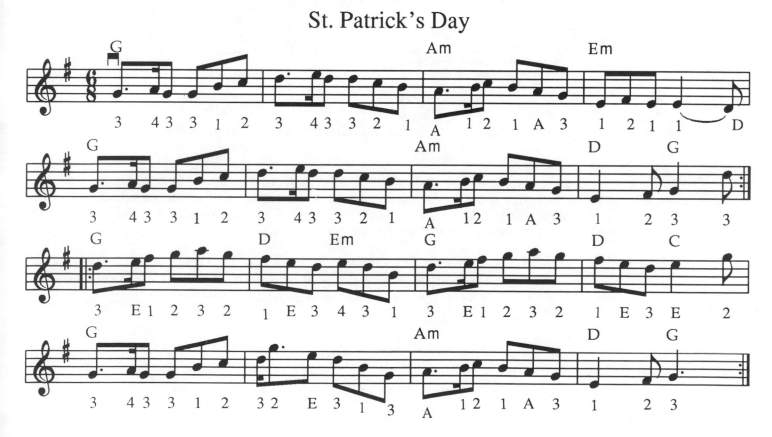

Lesson 36

This is another jig of Irish origin, played throughout North America. It is in the key of D and is played with a lilt.

Haste to the Wedding

Dorian Mode

Often fiddle tunes are played in a minor mode slightly different from the natural minor scale. One of the frequently used modes is the Dorian mode. This mode is made up of whole step, half step, whole step, whole step, whole step, half step, whole step. It is the same as starting on the second note of a major scale and playing that scale up one octave.

The next two tunes, both Irish jigs, have the key signature for the key of D. However, since the tunes are based around an E (the second note of the D major scale), they are actually in the Dorian mode.

The Road to Lisdoonvarna

Swallow Tail Jig

Photo by Charmaine Lanham

About the Author

Craig Duncan has written several books on fiddling for Mel Bay Publications, including *Deluxe Fiddling Method, Advanced Fiddling,* and *Top Fiddle Solos.* He works in the music business in Nashville, Tennessee, performing at numerous conventions, concerts, recordings, and private engagements. He has performed regularly on the Grand Ole Opry and The Nashville Network and is a member of the North American Fiddlers Hall of Fame. Along with performing, Craig is Artist/Teacher of Fiddle at Belmont College in Nashville. He is also proficient on the electric bass guitar, hammered dulcimer, and mandolin. Craig is married and has four children.

Acknowledgments

I want to thank Bill Bay for the opportunity to write this book and Charmaine Lanham for her photography. Thanks also go to Jay Vern and Jim Prendergast for their help on the recording that is available.